Q&A Kids

FORCES AND MAGNETS

AMY CHAPMAN
ANGELIKA SCUDAMORE

WINDMILL BOOKS

Published in 2026 by Windmill Books,
an Imprint of Rosen Publishing
2544 Clinton St.
Buffalo, NY 14224

First published in Great Britain in 2026
by Wayland

Editor: Sarah Peutrill
Designer: Lisa Peacock

Some of the text in this book was
first published in Fact Cat: Forces and
Magnets by Izzi Howell

Cataloging-in-Publication Data
Names: Chapman, Amy, author. | Scudamore, Angelika, illustrator.
Title: Forces and magnets / Amy Chapman, illustrated by Angelika Scudamore.
Description: Buffalo, NY : Windmill Books, 2026. | Series: Q & A kids | Includes glossary and index.
Identifiers: ISBN 9781725396197 (pbk.) | ISBN 9781725396203 (library bound) | ISBN 9781725396210 (ebook)
Subjects: LCSH: Force and energy--Juvenile literature. | Magnets--Juvenile literature.
Classification: LCC TJ163.23 C437 2026 | DDC 621.042--dc23

Printed in the United States of America

CPSIA Compliance Information: Batch #CSWM26
For Further Information contact Rosen Publishing
at 1-800-237-9932

CONTENTS

Can you spot this magnet in the book? There are 12 to find, not counting this one.

FORCES

Q. What are forces?

A. A force is a push or a pull.

Forces are at work all around you. You cannot see them, but you can see the effect they have on things. Stretching, squashing, twisting, and bending are all types of push or pull forces.

You use a pushing force on your bicycle pedals to make the wheels go around.

Forces even work inside your body. Your muscles pull on your bones to make you move.

FIND IT

Which force is each picture showing: stretching, squashing, twisting, or bending?

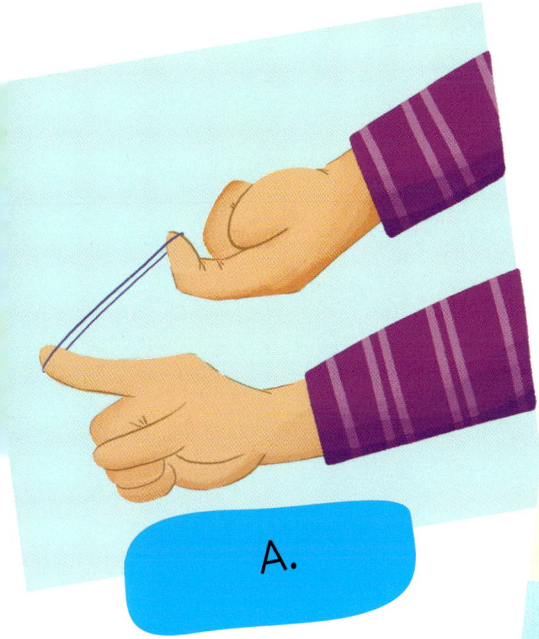
A.

B.

C.

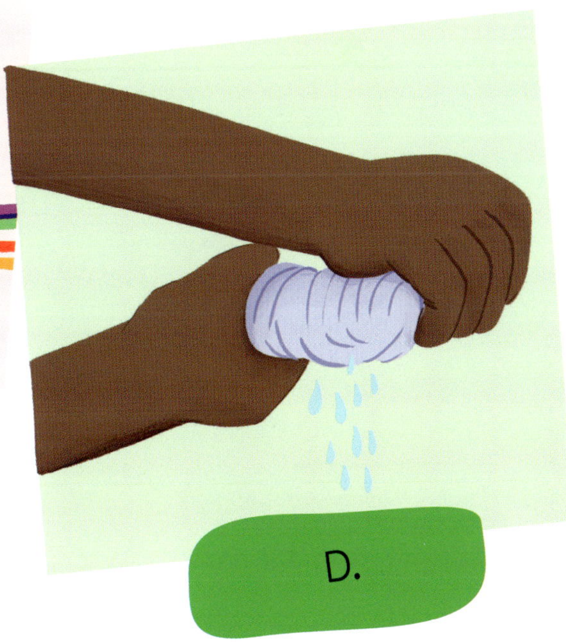
D.

STRONG OR WEAK

Q. Forces have to be strong, don't they?

A. No. Forces can be strong or weak. A strong push on a swing will make it go faster and higher than a weak push.

Think about an open door. If you touch it lightly, what will happen? It probably won't move very much. If you give it a big push, what will happen then? It will probably slam shut.

FIND IT

There are lots of pulling and pushing forces in this picture. How many can you find? Which do you think is the strongest and which is the weakest?

HOW FORCES WORK

Q. Do forces only make things go faster?

A. No. Forces can make things go faster, slower, or change an object's shape.

Forces affect objects in different ways. Pulling on a dog's leash will make them slow down. Pushing a toy car will make it speed up or change direction.

Forces can change the shape of objects. When you sit on a hopping ball, your weight pushes down and squashes it.

Forces work in pairs. If the forces are the same size, they cancel each other out. This means they do not change the way an object moves or change its shape.

If one force is bigger than another, an object will start moving, get faster, or change shape.

THINK ABOUT IT

The red team has an advantage and can pull more strongly. Which way will the teams move – toward A or B?

FRICTION

Q. Do forces help us?

A. Yes! There are many ways that forces are helpful to us. A force called friction helps you every day by stopping you from falling over!

Friction happens when two objects rub against each other. It always slows the objects down. Friction between your feet and the pavement stops you from slipping. To increase friction, some types of shoe have patterns in the sole. These grip the ground firmly when you walk or run.

Friction also stops these cars from sliding down the hill. And friction is what makes the wheels on the bike grip the ground as they turn.

THINK ABOUT IT

Friction also creates heat. What happens if you rub your hands together?

ROUGH AND SMOOTH

Q. Why can I skid in socks on a shiny floor but not on carpet?

A. Rough surfaces like carpet, gravel, or sandpaper create more friction than smooth surfaces. You can't slide across a rough carpet in the same way because there is more friction.

The smooth surface of snow creates hardly any friction, so it is good for skiing and sledding. We can design and make things that increase or decrease friction.

For example, an ice skate has a thin blade so it is easy to skate on ice. Soccer cleats have studs that help you to run on grass without slipping.

THINK ABOUT IT

Sara and Jo are each pushing a car forward. Which car do you think will travel the furthest? Why?

AIR RESISTANCE

Q. Does friction only happen between two hard surfaces?

A. No. Air resistance is a type of friction. It affects objects that are flying or falling. A lot of air resistance makes something fall more slowly.

Streamlined shapes reduce air resistance. Air flows more easily over long, thin shapes and smooth surfaces.

There is no air resistance in space because there is no air beyond Earth.

THINK ABOUT IT

As this parachute falls toward Earth, air resistance slows it down. Which direction does air resistance push?

WATER RESISTANCE

Q. Can you escape friction when you're in water?

A. No. When you swim, you can feel the force of the water pushing against you. This is a type of friction called water resistance.

Objects that are streamlined reduce water resistance. They have thin, pointy shapes that help them to move faster through water. Many fish have streamlined bodies.

Water resistance can be useful. If you want to move through water in a canoe or boat you can push against the water with oars.

THINK ABOUT IT

Why are some boats pointed at the front?

GRAVITY

Q. If something falls out of my pocket, does it land on the ground because of a push?

A. No. The object has been pulled to the ground by a force called gravity. It is a non-contact force, which means the objects don't have to touch for the effect to happen.

All the things you see around you are held on Earth by gravity. Big, heavy objects, like planets, have stronger gravity than lighter objects. Things fall toward Earth when they are dropped, because Earth's strong gravity pulls everything toward it.

FIND IT

Search the picture to find three things that are being pulled to the ground by gravity.

EARTH AND GRAVITY

Q. Does Earth's gravity just make things fall to the ground?

A. Earth's gravity pulls on the Moon just enough to keep it in orbit, but it is not strong enough to make the Moon crash into Earth.

The pull of gravity between the planets and the Sun keeps the solar system moving.

The rise and fall of the tides are caused by the gravity of the Sun and the Moon pulling on the sea.

THINK ABOUT IT

There is no gravity out in space. What would happen if this astronaut was not connected to the spacecraft?

MAGNETS

Q. What are magnets?

A. A magnet is anything that attracts magnetic objects. Most materials are not magnetic. For example, magnets do not attract paper, glass, wood, or plastic.

Some metals are magnetic, but not all of them are. Metals such as aluminium and copper are not magnetic.

Most forces affect objects only when they touch them. Gravity and magnetism affect objects without touching them.

SORT IT

We use different materials to make different things. Can you help Ollie sort out which of these objects are magnetic?

Aluminium foil
Steel paperclips
Wooden pencils
Wood plank
Iron nails
Plastic dominoes

TYPES OF MAGNET

Q. I have a horseshoe magnet. Are all magnets this shape?

A. Magnets come in many different shapes and sizes. For science experiments, you might use a bar magnet or a horseshoe magnet.

Small button magnets are strong enough to hold paper on a fridge (A) or to close a bag (B). Large magnets are strong enough to pick up big pieces of scrap metal (C).

Magnets are also used in computers and televisions. Some rollercoasters use magnets to get them started and help them slow down at the end of the ride.

THINK ABOUT IT

Why are the magnets useful on the bag?

A. Fridge magnets

B. Bag closer

C. Scrapyard magnet

NORTH AND SOUTH POLES

Q. Why do some magnets have different colored ends?

A. Sometimes we color magnets to show which pole is at each end. All magnets have a north pole and a south pole. Opposite poles attract each other. Two north poles or two south poles repel each other.

The north poles of these magnets are red and the south poles are blue. The arrows show how they push each other away (A) or pull together (B).

TRY IT

A force field is the area around a magnet that affects objects. With an adult, use tiny pieces of metal to see the shape of the force field around a magnet. Where is the force field strongest?

A.
S N
N S
B.
S N
S N

MAGNETIC EARTH

Q. What is the biggest magnet?

A. Actually, Earth is like a giant magnet! In the middle of Earth is a ball made of metal. This creates a huge magnetic force field around Earth as the planet spins. Earth's magnetic field is the same as a bar magnet (A).

Magnets on Earth are affected by its magnetic field. A magnet that can move freely will turn so that one end points toward the North Pole and the other toward the South Pole (B). Earth's magnetic field stretches nearly 37,000 miles (60,000 km) into space. That's one-fifth of the way to the Moon!

FIND OUT

The needle on a compass is magnetic. What are the four main points on a compass?

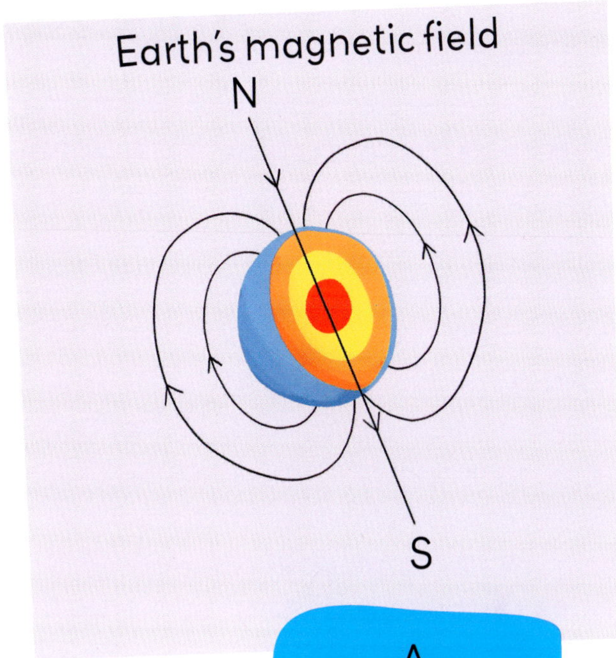

A.

B.

QUIZ

1. Which of these is a type of force?

a) sensing

b) stretching

c) saving

2. Smooth surfaces create more friction than rough surfaces. True or not true?

a) true

b) not true

3. Which force stops things on Earth from floating off into space?

a) friction

b) air resistance

c) gravity

4. All metals are magnetic. True or not true?

a) true

b) not true

5. The north pole of one magnet attracts the south pole of another magnet. True or not true?

a) true

b) not true

6. What type of force is caused by Earth's metal core?

a) magnetism

b) gravity

c) friction

Quiz answers:

1. b – stretching
2. b – not true
3. c – gravity
4. b – not true
5. a – true
6. a – magnetism

GLOSSARY

air resistance friction between an object and air

astronaut someone who goes into space

attract pull together

bar magnet a long, straight magnet, with poles at each end

bones the hard pieces that make up the solid frame of the body

compass a device that helps people travel in the right direction

direction the path that something moves along or the place it points to

force field the area where a force is at work

friction the force between two objects that are rubbing against each other

gravity a force that pulls objects together

horseshoe magnet a curved magnet, whose poles are close together

increase make bigger

magnetic something that is attracted to a magnet

magnetism the force that acts on magnetic materials

metals hard, shiny substances

muscles parts of the body attached to bones that stretch or shrink to make you move

orbit the path that objects in space move in around other objects

reduce make smaller

repel push apart

solar system the planets, including Earth, that move around the Sun

sole the bottom of a shoe

INDEX

SOME ANSWERS

p. 4 A. stretching; B. squashing; C. bending; D. twisting.
P. 6 Seven: pushing down on pedals; pushing (kicking) the football; pushing (blowing) the dandelion seeds; girl pulling a brush through her hair; dog pulling on the lead; man pushing the stroller.
p. 8 The teams will move toward B.
p. 10 Your hands feel warm if you rub them together.
p. 13 The blue car will travel furthest because the smooth floor creates less friction than the rug.
p. 14 Air resistance pushes up.
p. 16 The pointed shape helps a boat to cut through the water smoothly.
p. 18 The falling objects are: the football, the ice cream, and the leaf.
p. 20 The astronaut would float into space.
p. 22 Magnetic objects: steel paperclips and iron nails.
p. 24 The magnets help to close the bag tightly so nothing falls out.
p. 26 The force field is strongest near the poles.
p. 28 The four main points on a compass are: N (north), S (south), W (west) and E (east).